AF575529

BLUE Banner BIOGRAPHIES

# DEANDRE HOPKINS

Kerrily Sapet

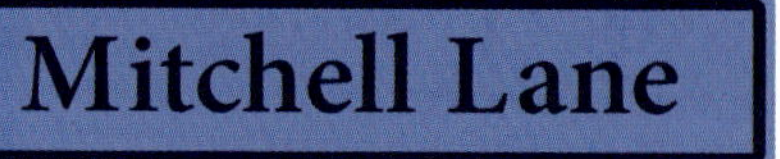

PUBLISHERS

mitchelllane.com

2001 SW 31st Avenue
Hallandale, FL 33009



First Edition, 2021.
Author: Kerrily Sapet
Designer: Ed Morgan
Editor: Morgan Brody

Series: Blue Banner Biographies
Title: DeAndre Hopkins / by Kerrily Sapet

Hallandale, FL : Mitchell Lane Publishers, [2021]

Library bound ISBN: 978-1-68020-623-4
eBook ISBN: 978-1-68020-624-1

PHOTO CREDITS: Design Elements, freepik.com, cover, pp. 5, 6, 9, 11, 13, 26 - Associated Press, p. 15 Charles Mitchell/Icon SMI. CFX/Charles Mitchell/Icon SMI./Newscom, p. 16 CURTIS COMPTON/MCT/Newscom, p. 19 Leslie Plaza Johnson/Icon Sportswire DBA/Leslie Plaza Johnson/Icon Sportswire/Newscom, p. 21 Troy Taormina-USA TODAY Sports TPX IMAGES OF THE DAY, p. 23 Maria Lysaker/ZUMA Press/Newscom, p. 25 Stephen Lew/Icon Sportswire DDN/Stephen Lew/Icon Sportswire/Newscom

# Contents

CHAPTER **ONE**

# The Accident

**DEANDRE HOPKINS** was running late as he drove through the heavy rainstorm towards "Death Valley." That grim nickname for Clemson University's stadium came from the old hillside cemetery that overlooked the field. A bus waited at the stadium to take DeAndre and his teammates to the airport. Their football team was flying to Florida to compete in the Orange Bowl. Rain poured from the sky, splatting against DeAndre's windshield and making deep pools on the road.

Focus and determination helped DeAndre Hopkins become a star wide receiver for the Houston Texans.

The car crash happened fast. DeAndre's tires skidded on the wet road and he lost control. His car spun across the highway, just missing oncoming traffic. It smashed into a tree. DeAndre hit his head hard. He woke up with his face in the mud and no idea how he got out of the car.

Jeff Scott, one of Clemson's coaches, saw the accident and recognized DeAndre's car. "I looked up in the tree and I could see the back of the car," Scott said. DeAndre escaped with a concussion. He was lucky—and he knew it! When DeAndre was a baby, his father had died in a car accident. His Uncle Russell also was killed in a crash. Tragedy haunted DeAndre's family.

# CHAPTER **ONE**

When DeAndre was a toddler, his cousin Louis died after suffering a heart attack during a basketball game. A few years later, his Uncle Terry, a professional football player, was killed during an act of domestic violence. When DeAndre was seven years old, his cousin Javis, DeAndre's idol, attempted suicide. Three years later, DeAndre's mother almost died after being attacked by another woman.

"[DeAndre] knew he definitely could have lost his life right there," said Scott. "It showed him how easily his life can be taken away from him." Although DeAndre was able to play in the Orange Bowl eight days later, his car accident changed him. DeAndre began to focus on what was important to him—family, education, and football, the sport he loved. He also started going to church and was baptized in a tub on Clemson's football field. After the accident, DeAndre played his best year of college football. Today, he is a star wide receiver for the Houston Texans in the National Football League (NFL).

DeAndre believes that the tragedies he experienced as a child helped him become the person he is today. "It all makes me so much stronger," DeAndre said. "I've been through so much . . . Nothing's too big to overcome." DeAndre has always pushed himself to play his hardest, to be a good teammate, and to help others. He knows that life can be short.

CHAPTER **TWO**

# Joys and Sorrows

**DEANDRE RASHAUN HOPKINS** was born on June 6, 1992 in Central, South Carolina. Five months later, his father, Harris Steve Hopkins, was killed in a car accident. DeAndre's mother, Sabrina, survived the crash but was left to care for their children by herself.

Sabrina worked several jobs to support her family. DeAndre had an older brother and sister, Marcus and Kesha, and a younger sister, Shanterria. DeAndre's family nicknamed him "Nuk"—after the one brand of pacifier DeAndre couldn't bite through.

Sabrina taught her children to be tough, to work hard, and to focus on the good things in life. We were a "tight family in a small house," DeAndre said. "We didn't really have much. We got what we needed, not what we wanted."

Despite their difficulties, they had happy times too. They celebrated holidays together and hunted for Easter eggs in the gardens nearby. DeAndre visited his great uncle outside of town, eating figs from a fig tree, and playing football in the backyard. A pine tree and a telephone pole marked the end zones. DeAndre was a natural athlete and a fierce competitor. At six years old, he could smack a baseball out of the park. "Nuk was a legend," said DeAndre's high school football coach Randy Robinson. "This kid was unbelievable."

Hopkins watches for a pass as the Houston Texans take on the San Diego Chargers in September 2019.

## CHAPTER **TWO**

When DeAndre was ten years old, his mother suffered life-threatening burns and was blinded when a jealous woman threw a mix of boiling chemicals at her. Scared and sad, DeAndre was too young to visit her in the hospital. After Sabrina came home, she didn't want to leave the house—until DeAndre asked her to one of his football games. "Mama, it doesn't matter as long as you're there," he said. Even though DeAndre's mother couldn't see him play, she asked others to lead her to the field. DeAndre learned from his mother as she grew stronger. "Nothing was going to stop me despite my challenges," he said. "That comes from my mom, her teaching me to have that willpower."

At D.W. Daniel High School, DeAndre played basketball and ran track. His friends talked him into joining the school's football team, too. As the team's wide receiver, DeAndre snagged passes in mid-air and racked up touchdowns. He used his basketball skills on the football field. "When the ball is up in the air for a rebound you always have to be on your toes to go up for the ball," he said. "It's the same situation in football as a receiver."

In DeAndre's senior year, he led the basketball team to their first state championship in years. He was also a star football player. In just three years, he caught 57 passes, intercepted 28 throws, and scored 23 touchdowns.

# Joys and Sorrows

In 2010, DeAndre accepted a scholarship from Clemson University to play football and basketball. The school was only five minutes from home. DeAndre wanted to help take care of his mother, even as he took the next step towards becoming a professional athlete.

Hopkins takes a shot as a guard on Clemson's basketball team.

CHAPTER THREE

# A Clemson Tiger

**DEANDRE HOPKINS** didn't just pick Clemson University because it was close to home. The school also had one of the best football programs in the country. More than 150 football players from Clemson had made it to the NFL. The school's legendary head coach, Dabo Swinney, was an expert at coaching wide receivers like Hopkins.

Hopkins makes a flying catch in a game against the Wake Forest Demon Deacons in November 2011.

Hopkins split his time between playing sports, attending classes, and studying. He worked hard and impressed his coaches and teammates. Hopkins had long arms and giant hands—10" from fingertip to thumb—helping him to reach difficult passes and grip the ball. To improve his catching speed, he studied flies when he was younger. "We always used to catch flies with our hands. I was the only one who could catch them," he said. "One-handed, two-handed . . . if I can catch that, I can catch anything."

# CHAPTER **THREE**

Hopkins played his first game against North Texas. The Clemson Tigers won the game and Hopkins had two catches. In a game the next week, he scored a touchdown. His success continued. By the end of the season, Hopkins had made 52 receptions and scored 4 touchdowns. "He's one of the most dominant players I've ever coached," said Dabo Sweeney. Hopkins decided to stop playing basketball so he could focus on football.

Hopkins continued to dominate on the field for the next two years. In his junior year, he had one of the best receiving seasons ever in Atlantic Coast Conference history. He made 82 catches and scored 18 touchdowns—the most ever by a Clemson player. At the Orange Bowl in January 2013, he grabbed 13 passes and scored 2 touchdowns, helping Clemson defeat Louisiana State University. Hopkins was ranked the second-best receiver in the country.

## A Clemson Tiger

Hopkins catches a pass to help Clemson defeat LSU in December 2012.

# CHAPTER **THREE**

Hopkins gets past LSU safety Eric Reid for a touchdown reception.

# A Clemson Tiger

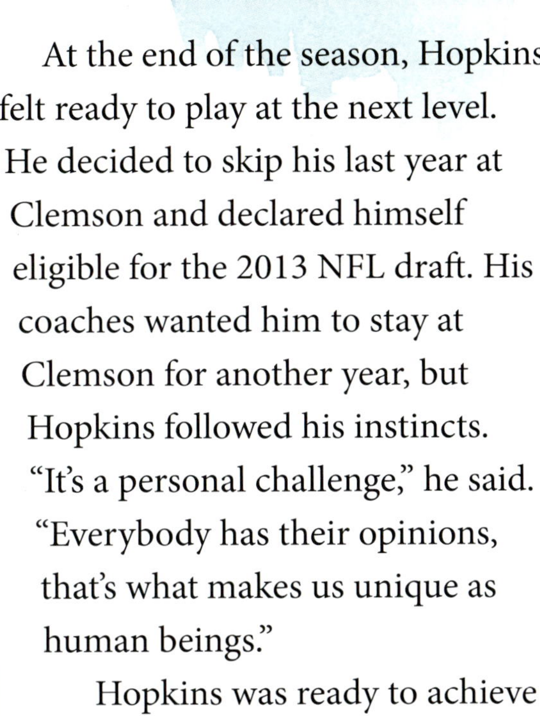

At the end of the season, Hopkins felt ready to play at the next level. He decided to skip his last year at Clemson and declared himself eligible for the 2013 NFL draft. His coaches wanted him to stay at Clemson for another year, but Hopkins followed his instincts. "It's a personal challenge," he said. "Everybody has their opinions, that's what makes us unique as human beings."

Hopkins was ready to achieve his dream of playing in the NFL. Recruiters and coaches had been watching him for years. NFL teams were waiting.

CHAPTER FOUR

# Achieving a Dream

**AS THE DRAFT** approached, DeAndre Hopkins attended workouts with NFL teams and competed in the NFL Scouting Combine, a series of drills and tests. On April 25, 2013, the Houston Texans picked Hopkins in the first round of the draft. He signed a four-year contract for $7.62 million and moved to Houston, Texas, nearly 1,000 miles away from home.

Hopkins began practicing with the team and learning their playbook. He memorized hundreds of plays such as "0 Flood Flank FIP R-34 Flash A Shark." The plays, written in a jumbled code, gave the players directions on the field.

Hopkins also learned from Andre Johnson, the Texans' starting wide receiver. "One thing that I appreciate about him [Hopkins] is when he first came into the league, he asked me about things he needed to do to better his game," said Johnson. "He took that to a whole other level."

Hopkins played his first NFL game in the season opener against the San Diego Chargers. His four receptions helped the Texans win the game. In his next game, Hopkins scored his first NFL touchdown. By the end of the season, Hopkins had caught 52 passes and scored 2 touchdowns. He continued to improve. In one game, he scored a 76-yard touchdown and made a spectacular one-handed catch to help defeat the Washington Redskins. Hopkins soon set a team record for scoring the most touchdowns in one season.

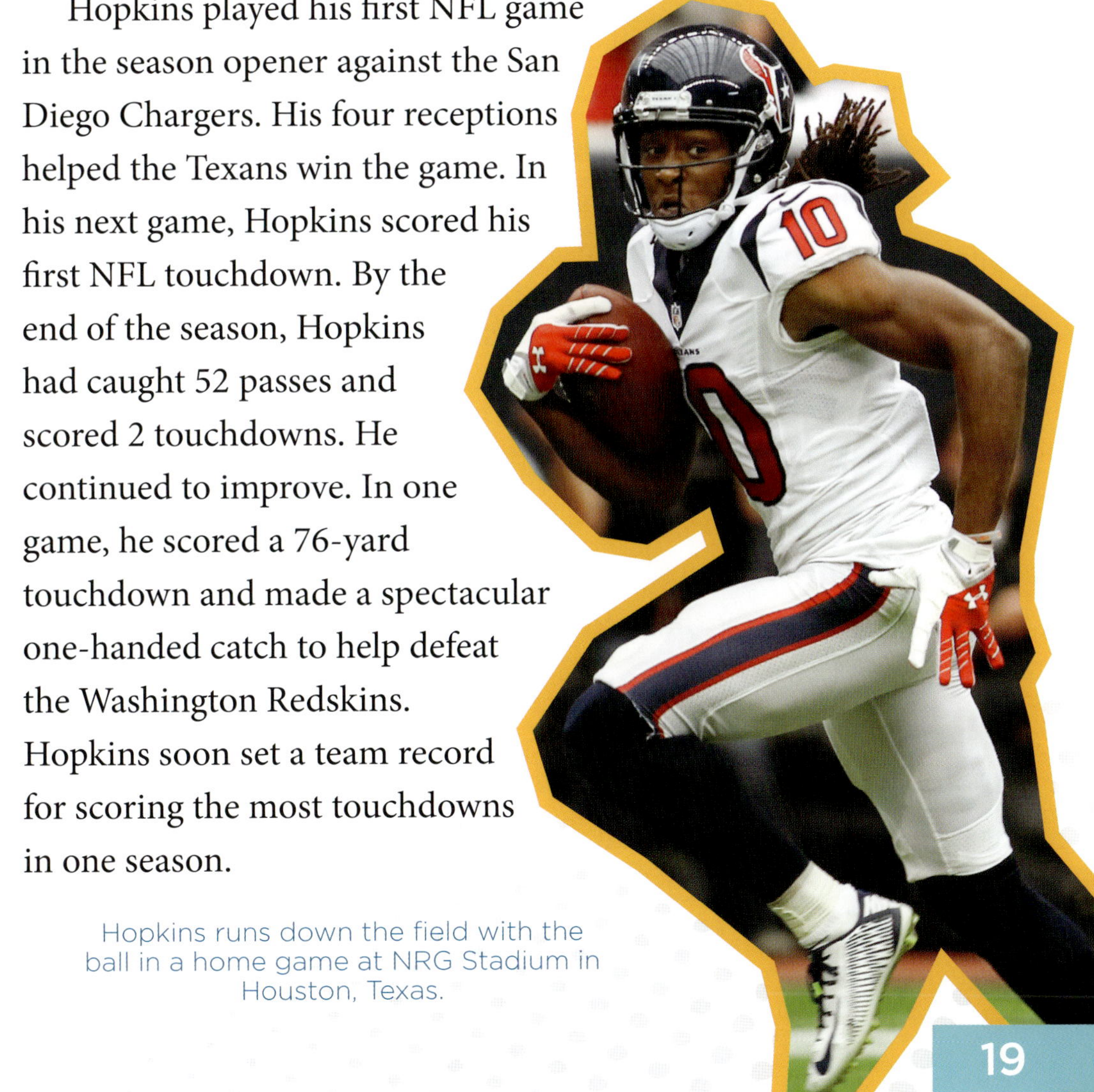

Hopkins runs down the field with the ball in a home game at NRG Stadium in Houston, Texas.

# CHAPTER **FOUR**

Hopkins worked hard on and off the field. "D-Hop's a special guy because of his competitive nature, his work ethic," said John Perry, one of the DeAndre's coaches. Hopkins watched videotapes of plays to help him improve. He became the first receiver in NFL history to catch 110 passes with 0 drops. "He has the best hands in the world," said Perry.

With his acrobatic catches, Hopkins amazed fans and players. They wondered; *How did he do that?* Hopkins especially appreciated the praise from other players. "I take pride in my work," he said. "For them to say that, it's an honor because those guys put in as much work as I do."

Hopkins also proved his talent by working with nine different starting quarterbacks in just four years. In 2017, the Texans drafted Deshaun Watson as their new quarterback. Hopkins and Watson, who also attended Clemson, quickly became friends and made a tough duo to beat on the field. "D-Hop's . . . like my brother," said Watson.

In August 2017, Hopkins signed a five-year contract for $81 million to continue playing for the Texans, making him the highest paid wide receiver in the NFL. Hopkins was also one of the greatest.

Hopkins attempts to make a reception, catching the ball between his legs, in a game against the Miami Dolphins.

CHAPTER **FIVE**

# A Texas Star

**IN 2019, DEANDRE HOPKINS** was named the 11th best player in the NFL. Throughout his career with the Houston Texans, he has only missed one game—despite injuring his thumb, ankle, foot, and hamstring muscle. His worst injury occurred in 2019 during a Super Bowl playoff game against the Indianapolis Colts. Hopkins sprained a joint in his shoulder, tearing ligaments off the bone. He still caught five passes.

Hopkins receives a pass during a playoff game between the Houston Texans and the Indianapolis Colts in January 2019.

"It's the most banged up I've ever been playing football," Hopkins said. "I was dealing with serious injuries . . . But we had a good team that depended on me, and I never gave a thought to not playing unless the doctors told me I couldn't."

# CHAPTER **FIVE**

Hopkins pushes himself to overcome his injuries, like his mother. After nearly 40 eye surgeries, she has regained some of her sight. She still can't see Hopkins when he plays, but she comes to his games. His sister Kesha, who also lives in Houston, plays for the Houston Wildcats, a women's football league. Hopkins also has a young daughter.

Family is important to Hopkins, and so is helping other people. He remembers the tough times in his childhood. Hopkins and his mother founded a charity, called SMOOOTH, to help victims of domestic violence. SMOOOTH stands for Speaking Mentally Outwardly Opening Opportunities Towards Healing. Each year, they give away backpacks filled with school supplies to thousands of children. "We just wanted to give back to the community that did so much for us growing up . . . it was only right to do something to give back," Hopkins said. "It's the best feeling to be able to give back."

Hopkins stretches to make the catch as Marshon Lattimore of the New Orleans Saints attempts a tackle.

# A Texas Star

# CHAPTER **FIVE**

Hopkins stops to greet fans after a game against the New York Jets.

# A Texas Star

Hopkins helps out at food banks, donates money, hosts football camps for young players, and purchases football equipment for youth football teams. Not only is Hopkins one of the NFL's best receivers, he uses his fame and fortune to help others. DeAndre Hopkins is a true star.

# Timeline

**1992** DeAndre Rashaun Hopkins is born on June 6 in Central, South Carolina.

**2002** DeAndre's mother suffers a near-fatal attack and is blinded.

**2010** Hopkins leads his high school basketball team to a state championship; he begins attending Clemson University.

**2012** Hopkins sets an Atlantic Coast Conference record, scoring 18 touchdowns.

**2013** Hopkins is drafted by the Houston Texans in the first round of the NFL Draft.

**2014** Hopkins and his mother found the charitable organization SMOOOTH.

**2017** Hopkins is the NFL leader in number of receiving touchdowns.

**2019** Hopkins is ranked 11th in the Top 100 Players of 2019.

## Career Stats

| | |
|---|---|
| Total Games Played | 95 |
| Total Games Won | 44 |
| Total Games Lost | 51 |
| Total Touchdowns Scored | 47 |
| Total Receptions | 528 |
| Total Receiving Yards | 7,437 |
| Total Fumbles | 7 |

# Find Out More

## Books

The Editors of Sports Illustrated. *Football: Then to WOW! (Sports Illustrated Kids Then to WOW!)*. New York, NY: Sports Illustrated Kids, 2016.

Gramling, Gary. *The Football Fanbook: Everything You Need to Become a Gridiron Know-it-All*. New York, NY: Sports Illustrated Kids, 2015.

Whiting, Jim. *Houston Texans*. Mankato, MN: Creative Paperbacks, 2019.

## On the Internet

DeAndre Hopkins Stats
https://www.houstontexans.com/team/players-roster/deandre-hopkins/

DeAndre Hopkins Details, News, and Videos
https://www.espn.com/nfl/player/_/id/15795/deandre-hopkins

# Works Consulted


Barshop, Sarah. "Texans DeAndre Hopkins Never Satisfied in Quest 'For Greatness.'" ESPN, August 5, 2019. https://www.espn.com/blog/houston-texans/post/_/id/23850/texans-deandre-hopkins-never-satisfied-in-quest-for-greatness

Duncan, Avery. "Texans WR DeAndre Hopkins Caught Flies as a Kid to Train His Hands." *Texans Wire*, August 13, 2019. https://texanswire.usatoday.com/2019/08/13/texans-wr-deandre-hopkins-flies-train-hands/

Ganguli, Tania. "For Hopkins, Survival Has Been the Name of the Game." *Houston Chronicle*, May 4, 2013. https://www.houstonchronicle.com/sports/texans/article/For-Hopkins-survival-has-been-the-name-of-the-4489168.php

Houston Texans website. https://www.houstontexans.com

Jackson, Vince. "Hopkins 'Thankful' to Give Back to Community." *Independent Mail*, June 13, 2015. http://archive.independentmail.com/sports/college/clemson/hopkins-thankful-to-give-back-to-community-ep-1135128966-348408851.html

Kasabian, Paul. "DeAndre Hopkins Played Through Serious Shoulder Injury in Texans' Playoff Loss." *Bleacher Report*, June 8, 2019. https://bleacherreport.com/articles/2840156-deandre-hopkins-played-through-serious-shoulder-injury-in-texans-playoff-loss

Keepfer, Scott. "Former Clemson Star Receiver Catches His Breath at Home." *Greenville News*, July 22, 2017. https://www.greenvilleonline.com/story/sports/college/clemson/2017/07/22/former-clemson-star-receiver-catches-his-breath-home/501701001/

Keepfer, Scott. "Single-Mom Success: Greenlee Ran 'Tight Ship' at Home." *Greenville News*, July 9, 2016. https://www.greenvilleonline.com/story/sports/college/clemson/2016/07/09/single-mom-success-greenlee-ran-tight-ship-home/86791108/

Klemko, Robert. "NFL Prospect DeAndre Hopkins Steeled by Tragedies." *USA Today*, April 15, 2013. https://www.usatoday.com/story/sports/nfl/2013/04/15/deandre-hopkins-nfl-draft-many-tragedies/2086501/

McClain, John. "It's Just Practice, but DeAndre Hopkins Can Put on a Show." *Houston Chronicle*, August 1, 2019. https://www.houstonchronicle.com/sports/columnists/mcclain/article/It-s-just-practice-but-DeAndre-Hopkins-can-put-14274630.php

# Index



# About the Author

Kerrily Sapet is the author of more than 25 books for children and numerous magazine articles. She has written biographies ranging in topics from queens to writers to race car drivers. Sapet grew up in the heart of Pittsburgh Steelers territory. Although she has visited Houston, Texas, she has never seen DeAndre Hopkins play.